AF567089

Graphology

Dear Fran

How are you? I hope you are fine. And How is Barabra? I hopes shes fine too. Tell Earl hello and to send me his address. I'm sure mom would Dad and I would to make good use of it. My birthday is April 28, 1970. In French it is Abril 28, 1971. Plese send me a nice present. Tell Earl to send one too. Some poems I've just learned I want you to hear. They start on back.

Tiger my cat

Tiger is about seven months old. We found him when he was a kitten. He was a wild cat. My mother was really against the idea because she thought we wouldn't look after him But, after a while everyone liked him and we kept him for good. He is a very playful cat.

skateboardigs

Over 3,000,000 kids ride them today. They range in price from $10.00 to $80.00. abouts 30 kids ride them in my school. We have a speshle plase to ride in the parking lot. there are many stunts like skiping and welays. and skateboarding is very fun

How have you been? I am doing great. I have a new boyfriend. His name is David. He'll be up your way next week. How's Melvin or whoever it is now? By the way, who is it. How's Mario? Tell him hello.

I am really exicited about starting school. We start on Sept 23. I am getting a grant for $326 and I have about $300 savings and I am suppposed to get some more aid from the school so I hope to go to school off that. It comes to about 900 so I may have enough saved from the fall & winter to pay for the Spring quarter without borrowing any money. I refuse to go to the Credit Union. I don't think Mom and Dad will have to give me more than $150 dollars. I HOPE. That's my big news.

How's your job considering your hands a broken? Miss & Love you a whole Lot. Write Soon (smile).

Graphology

A Guide to Handwriting Analysis

BY THOMAS G. AYLESWORTH

FRANKLIN WATTS | NEW YORK | LONDON | 1976

Photographs courtesy of: Spanish National Tourist Office: p. xii; The Metropolitan Museum of Art: p. 4; Swedish Information Service: p. 3; Smithsonian Office of Anthropology, Bureau of American Ethnology Collection: p. 8.

Library of Congress Cataloging in Publication Data

Aylesworth, Thomas G
Graphology : a guide to handwriting analysis.

(A Concise guide)
Bibliography: p.
Includes index.
SUMMARY: A description of how to analyze handwriting to reveal the personality of the writer.
1. Graphology—~~Juvenile literature. [1. Graphology~~] I. Title.
BF891.A9 137'.7 76-7048
ISBN 0-531-00323-X

Printed in the United States of America
5 4 3 2 1

Contents

Special thanks to
James Bardner,
Doug O'Brien,
Andrea Walker,
Josephine Walker,
Sandy Walker,
and Sandra Walker
for permission
to use their
handwriting samples.

OTHER BOOKS BY THE AUTHOR

The Alchemists: Magic into Science
Astrology and Foretelling the Future
Cars, Boats, Trains, and Planes of Today and Tomorrow
ESP
Into the Mammal's World
It Works Like This
Monsters from the Movies
Movie Monsters
Mysteries from the Past
Palmistry
The Search for Life
Servants of the Devil
Teaching for Thinking (with Gerald Reagan)
This Vital Air, This Vital Water
Traveling into Tomorrow
Vampires and Other Ghosts
Werewolves and Other Monsters
Who's Out There?
The World of Microbes

For Don and Joan Allen
Two dear friends who
never use a typewriter

Graphology

A bison drawn on the rock wall of a cave in Spain. The artist was a prehistoric human. Scientists don't agree on what to call cave drawings—art, hunting magic, or writing.

Graphology: What Is It?

Writing is a strange and wondrous thing. And it has a long history. People have been using written symbols for over six thousand years. This probably started in the area of Mesopotamia, Assyria, Babylonia, and Persia.

In the ancient societies, writing was a holy thing. After all, it was a way of changing the sounds of speech into visible forms. That sounds like magic, so the ancient peoples thought that writing must have been invented by the gods. Add to this the fact that the priests were usually the only ones who could do it, and writing got a big reputation.

The Egyptians used picture writing inside their tombs and called it "the speech of the gods." The Greeks called the Egyptian letters **hieroglyphics**, or "sacred carvings."

These hieroglyphics were magic to the Egyptians. The marks were not just pictures, they were the thing itself. For example, suppose that a hieroglyph for a bird had to be used in a tomb. What if the bird ate the store of grain that was being left for the dead person to use in the afterworld? More than that, what if the bird ate the dead body? The Egyptians thought that this was possible, so they figured out a way of preventing it. Sometimes they used an incomplete drawing of the bird. At other times they might draw the bird in two separate halves. In this way, they believed, the whole animal could not appear.

RUNES

In northern Europe during the early centuries of the Christian era, there were magic letters called **runes**. This term came from a word meaning "mystery," or "secret." The modern German word *raunen,* for example, means "to whisper." Runes were used inside a tomb to keep evil spirits away from the body or to prevent the body from leaving the burial place. This is another example of the belief that writing is powerful.

Here is a quote from an early Swedish gravestone, written in runes: "This is the meaning of the runes; I hid here magic runes undisturbed by evil witchcraft. He who destroys this monument shall die in misery by magic art."

Runes were used on weapons, too. One warrior named his sword "Marr," and wrote on it, "May Marr spare nobody."

Runes were said to be able to bring the dead back to life. This is from an old poem:

> A twelfth spell I know; when I see aloft upon a tree
> A corpse swinging from a rope.
> Then I cut and paint runes
> So that the man walks
> And speaks with me.

Runes carved on a stone in Gripsholm, Sweden.

An old legend says that Odin, the chief god of the Germanic peoples of northern Europe, wanted to learn the mysteries of the runes. To do this he had to hang for nine days and nights with a spear sticking through his body into Yggdrasil, the tree of life. When his torture was over, he seized the runes, saying:

I peered downwards,
I took up the runes,
Screaming, I took them—
Then I fell back.

When northern Europe became Christian, the early priests outlawed the writing of runes. There was too much of a connection between these markings and pagan religions and magic. In Iceland, as late as the seventeenth century, people were burned at the stake if they were caught with some runes.

EARLY WRITING

In a way, writing goes back further than just to the ancient tribes of the Middle East. Drawings dating back to 20,000 B.C. have been found on the walls of caves. Not only were there pictures of animals and humans, but there were also geometric shapes and patterns. They are thought to have religious and magical significance.

So writing, as we know it, seems to have come through three main stages. The first was the **pictograph** type of writ-

The pharaoh Akhenaton and Queen Nefertiti of Egypt making an offering to the sun god, Aton. The symbols in columns above their heads are hieroglyphics.

ing. If you wanted to write the word "sun," you drew a picture of the sun like this:

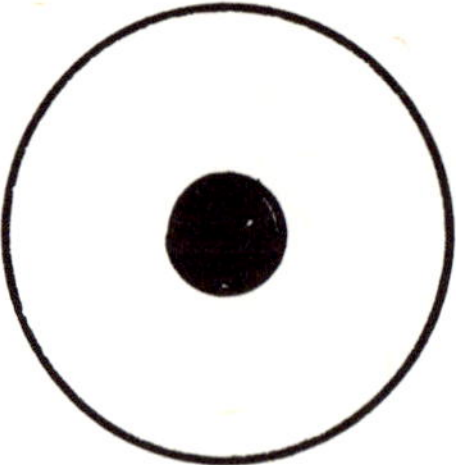

Want to write "star"? Just draw

The next type of writing was the **ideograph**. Take the picture for the sun in the last paragraph. In ideographic writing, the drawing means not only the sun but also some of its characteristics. "Light," "heat," "brightness," and "day" are examples of these new meanings. The picture of the star may also refer to heaven, or even God.

Ideographic writing is complicated. When you see a picture of the sun, how do you know whether it means "day" or "hot"? The drawing can have several different meanings. And then there is the problem of abstractions. How would you draw a picture of the words "truth" or "justice"?

The answer, of course, is the phonetic type of writing, such as we use now. Here we have symbols that stand for sounds, not things. We have twenty-six symbols in English—called the alphabet. Other Western languages have about the same number, give or take a few.

Many scholars think that all of the alphabets of the world are descendants of one original alphabet. This first alphabet was probably invented in either Syria or Palestine sometime between 1750 and 1500 B.C.

GRAPHOLOGY— THE BEGINNING

We no longer think that writing is a magic thing, but there are many people who think that handwriting can communicate much more than ideas. It can tell us, some believe, something about the personality of the writer, his or her physical and mental state, and a little about the subject's future. The technique of reading these things from handwriting is called **graphology.**

Graphology probably started about 1000 B.C. in China and Japan. We know that one of the most famous early believers was the Greek philosopher Aristotle. He once wrote that he could "define the soul of people by their way of writing."

During the Middle Ages, Catholic monks practiced the art. Later, Shakespeare wrote: "Give me the handwriting of a woman, and I will tell you her character." That's not as easy to do today, as will be explained later.

The first known book on graphology was published in Florence, Italy, in 1622. The author was Camillo (or Camilio) Baldi, and the title of the book was *De signis ex epistolis* (rough translation: "The Meaning of Letters"). It had a subtitle: "Treating of How a Written Message May Reveal the Nature of Qualities of the Writer." Baldi was a professor of medicine, philosophy, and logic at the University of Bologna. He traveled around from castle to castle analyzing the writing of the lords and ladies.

By the way, it might seem strange that the first book on graphology was written only a little more than three hundred years ago. That isn't very long, considering that, for example,

The scenes painted on this
buffalo skin are picture writing.
They tell the life story
of an important Pawnee chief.

palmistry books were printed in the 1400s. But remember that handwriting is a rather recent invention. At least, it has not been too long that being able to write was a fairly common thing. And people have always had palms.

During the eighteenth century, graphology was, for the most part, treated as a parlor game. It didn't really get off the ground as a serious study until the middle of the nineteenth century. It was then that Abbé Jean-Hippolyte Michon, a Frenchman, developed a set of handwriting signs. He included the different kinds of loops, the various kinds of crossings of the letter *t,* the dottings of the letter *i,* and so on. He then arranged these signs according to mental traits.

Graphology as an art blossomed. Some of the people who were believers were such authors and poets as Goethe, Robert Browning, Elizabeth Barrett Browning, George Sand, Baudelaire, Balzac, Sir Walter Scott, and Sir Arthur Conan Doyle. The author Guy de Maupassant said: "Dark words on white paper bare the soul." Edgar Allan Poe actually analyzed handwriting and published his findings. Others who were enthusiastic about graphology were Vincent van Gogh, the artist; Felix Mendelssohn, the composer, and Benjamin Disraeli, the prime minister of Britain.

GRAPHOANALYST

Today, the truly professional analyst is called a **graphoanalyst**. He or she has been certified by the International Graphoanalysis Society. The society has trained 35,000 people to be graphoanalysts in the last forty-six years. The training takes eighteen months. At the present time, there are about 9,000 trained people active in the field. Most of them are used by business and industry as consultants. But many of them help police departments and other law enforcement bodies in searching out forgeries.

Obviously, one of the regrets that the society has is that

there are hundreds of thousands of people who claim to be experts in graphology. They give the properly trained grapho-analyst a bad name. In defense of the society, its president, V. Peter Ferrara, says: "It [graphoanalysis] is as scientific and accurate as any other psychological test. It's probably more precise than the Rorschach [inkblot] Test. It's as good as the best and no worse than many. I know that's a negative way to describe it, but it's brutally true. Some people complain that no psychological tests are accurate."

Some amazing things have come out of the work of grapho-analysis. Some graphoanalysts have been able to diagnose health problems from a study of handwriting. The American Medical Association included the following in one of its reports: "There are definite organic diseases that grapho-diagnostics can help to diagnose from their earliest beginnings."

Obviously, those diseases that cause a trembling of the hands, such as Parkinson's disease, would be included. But the American Medical Association also included anemia, blood poisoning, tumors, and some bone diseases in their list. And there is a dermatologist in Hawaii who uses graphoanalysis to figure out the causes of skin eruptions. If the cause is psycho-logical, it could show up in the patient's handwriting.

Now you have a brief summary of the state of graphology —past and present. But you are not ready to read and analyze handwriting yet. There are a few things to understand before you start.

Some Words of Caution

Most people—even those who do not believe in graphology—think that they can tell a lot about a painter by looking at his or her paintings. They feel that they can sense if the painter is male or female. They certainly know a great deal about his or her interests because of what subject matter is to be found in the paintings.

And what is handwriting but a drawing? Also, it is a drawing that speaks to us. So it may have two meanings. One meaning consists of the words that are written. The other meaning is what the writer unconsciously tells us about his or her personality through the shape of the writing.

Even those people who reject the opinions of the graphologist must consider a few things. Almost everyone will have to admit that a lazy person will have lazy handwriting. Neat persons will have neat handwriting. In a way, writing is a form of body language.

When you are reading a person's handwriting, you may want to pay attention to the **punctuation** of the writing. Some graphologists do. If the punctuation is good, they say, the subject is orderly and logical. If bad, the subject is very active and may be very intelligent.

Another thing that you may or may not want to pay attention to is the **margination** of the page. A few graphologists feel that this is important. Most of them, however, think that every writer varies in his or her margins. Sometimes our margins are wide, sometimes they are narrow. It often has something to do with how much we have to say. For example, if you have to write a three-page paper for school and don't have much to say, your margins may be large. If you have to say a lot on a postcard, you may not use any margins at all.

One more thing that you can take a choice about is the **paper** used. Is it clean or dirty, spotless or blotted? Some graphologists feel that this tells something about the writer. Others believe that a messy paper may just show the writer thinks that paper should not be wasted.

LEARN ABOUT YOUR SUBJECT

There are a few things that can throw off your analysis. **Age** is one. It is rather important to have a general idea about the subject's age. At least you should know whether he or she is a child or a grown-up. Children's writing normally has letters that get larger toward the end of each word. If an adult's writing does this, it may be a sign of childishness.

You also may want to know something about the eyesight of the subject. Many nearsighted people write small, and many farsighted people write large. This may, therefore, not be a sign of any mental characteristic. It might just mean that the subject needs glasses.

There are some other things that can mess up your analysis unless you know about them beforehand. Think about your own handwriting. Does it change when you are pushed for time? In a bad temper? Using a new pen or pencil? Excited? Sad? Thinking of something more important? Of course it does.

Other things that can affect handwriting are old age, sickness, and nervousness. Just sitting in an uncomfortable chair can influence writing, as can a desk that is too high or too low, a bad light, a temperature that is too high or too low, or any number of other uncomfortable situations.

There are a couple of other things that you should learn about your subject. Even trained graphologists will admit that they cannot be sure about people from looking at a sample of handwriting.

The first is knowing whether the subject is **right-** or **left-handed.** This may sound simple to you, but the experts have to ask.

The second is knowing whether the subject is a **man** or a **woman.** That's right. There was a time when the female writer had a repressed handwriting, as Shakespeare noted. They were taught to write differently from males—in an angular fashion. Also, their handwriting was lighter than that of men. And they sometimes thought of cute things to do, such as dotting their *i*'s with little circles. But by and large this is no longer true. Over the last thirty years, the experts have been having more and more trouble in separating male from female handwriting.

COLLECTING SAMPLES

Now we have to get to some things that you must remember if you want to analyze writing. First, it is important to realize that everyone's handwriting is, in one way or another, a learned thing. We are not born with it. Our writing shows the effects of the efforts of our teachers, our own ideas of what good handwriting is, and the job writing does for us.

Think back. Probably everyone has experimented with a

change in his or her handwriting at some time or another. We all know people who print their capital letters even though all the rest of their letters are written, not printed. Little circles over the *i*'s have been mentioned. Some people use the Greek *e* (ℰ) rather than the normal *e* (ℯ).

After you have settled on your handwriting, it usually becomes automatic. You don't think about it anymore. What happens is that the pen or pencil seems to have a mind of its own. At the point where there is little conscious concern about how the writing looks, the expression of the writer's character can slip in.

The serious graphologist must collect several samples of the subject's writing. Ideally, these should be produced at different times and with different pens.

The collecting must be done on the sly. A piece of writing created to be analyzed is almost useless. The subject may be showing off or trying to disguise some of his or her traits. And in almost all cases, the subject will be too self-conscious about his or her writing to give you a typical sample. Some graphologists feel that the ideal sample is made up of two whole pages of the subject's unsuspecting efforts—even then you throw away the first page of the sample.

Another thing to look for is consistency. Be sure that the characteristics of the writing are repeated over and over again. One time is not enough—it might be just a slip of the pen.

Here's another big job for you. Be careful to separate those characteristics that were learned from those characteristics that the subject has developed.

Here is an example. Perhaps you know some people who make their figure 7 like this: 7 . That may look like an affectation to you. But if the subject had learned to write in Europe, it would be the normal way of writing a 7. What may seem to be a way of calling attention to the person's handwriting was merely the normal way of writing—just as he or she was taught in school.

Two other examples. Long up-and-down strokes may merely mean that the subject learned to write in France. Extra-heavy lines may only mean that the subject was using paper of poor quality or a felt-tip pen.

Now you are ready to collect your samples. Remember to be sure that they are real and not disguised. Since we all disguise our handwriting from time to time, here is a list of things not to use in analysis:

1. Don't use hastily written samples. They do not really reflect the subject's true writing.
2. Don't use a sample with just a few words on it. Your subject may have been too careful in writing.
3. Don't, if possible, use a sample written in pencil. The pen is usually much more sensitive.
4. Don't use postcard samples. They are usually too crowded and pinched, and the spacing of the lines is very important in graphology.
5. Don't use a sample that has been written to someone in power, such as a teacher or a boss. These are usually too carefully written in order not to reveal the real character of the writer.
6. Don't use a sample that is a copy of something that someone else has written—a Bible verse, for example. The writer may not really believe what he or she has written, and the writing will be unconsciously changed.

So much for the DON'Ts. Remember the one big DO. Do try to get a sample of writing that the subject does not know will be used for analysis. A letter written to a friend is ideal, since one is really trying to put oneself into the writing, and should be more honest than usual—both in what is said and in how it is written.

Now, keeping in mind that handwriting should be studied as a whole, not as a bunch of symbols, you are ready to learn to analyze. Deep down, everyone is a graphologist. If you have ever received a love letter, you know what that means. Unconsciously, you consider the handwriting of your friend to be a secret message. What else can be more upsetting than to get a love note that is typed?

Quick-Glance Graphology

You can learn a lot about a person in a short period of time by using a "quick-glance" method of graphology. It doesn't tell the whole story, of course. But it tells a good part of it. In this method, you are looking at the obvious traits of the handwriting—the lines of writing, the size of writing, the angles of writing, and the spacing of the lines and letters. It can give you some general ideas about the personality of the writer.

LINES OF WRITING

The first thing to do is look at the lines of writing. Do they turn up or down? Are they level or bowed?

Let's start out with the level lines that go straight across the paper. Here we have a person with a will of iron, who is determined to succeed, and probably is mentally well balanced. But the subject can also be unreasonable and very demanding of others. To tell whether the writer is reasonable or

On behalf of Green Vale School and the Parents Association, I should like to express our great appreciation

level lines

unreasonable, look at the writing itself. If it is relaxed, you have an honest but not dominating person. If it is rigid, it means just the opposite, so look out.

The subject can also write with a level line that has a bit of wandering along the line. Here, as you would expect, you have a person who is a little off balance. Not that the person is mentally unbalanced, but rather careless and changeable.

We deeply appreciated your willingness to share your time and talent with us again this year.

wandering lines

In short, the writer is a weak person. On the other hand, if the wanderings are minor, you may be faced with a genius. Or, at least, here is a person who has many talents in many different directions.

Suppose that the lines have an upward slant. Here is someone with ambition. The subject is optimistic and physically active. But this is not necessarily good, because the per-program scored 100%, and the classroom question and answer period was

upward slant

son can also be sloppy, stupid, and vain. And there is a tendency to boast, brag, and lie about his or her abilities. If the slant is slight, the subject has more self-control. You can make a bit of a generalization here. The higher the slant, the bigger the ego.

Downward slanting tells of a moody person. Also, it says that here is a person who can easily be discouraged. Once again, the bigger the slant, the stronger the trait. That is, the bigger, the moodier. A slight downward line just means that the subject does not spend time being unnecessarily enthusiastic.

Some day I would like to be a writer or a poet.

downward slant

One thing you must be careful of here. Some people, because they are ill or tired, may let their lines slant downward just because of exhaustion. This doesn't necessarily mean that they are moody. On the other hand, if the illness or weariness is extreme, it might cause them to be pessimistic and moody. So you have to be careful in your analysis.

Basically, of course, either lines are level or they slant up or down. But let's look at some combinations of these.

1. If the writing is level, then rises at the end of the line, the subject is basically optimistic, but will wait until the proper time to show enthusiasm. Here is a strong person that you can depend on.
2. If the writing is level, but slants downward at the end of the line, the subject is weak and worried. But he or she may be merely tired, so be careful in this analysis.
3. If the writing is humped—rising toward the middle of the line and falling toward the end of the line—the subject is changeable. Here is a person who often starts a job with enthusiasm, then gives up too soon.
4. If the writing is dipped—falling toward the middle of the line and rising toward the end of the line—you have the opposite. This person starts a job without much enthusiasm, but gets excited once involved in it.

SIZE OF WRITING

We all know that some people's writing is huge, while other people's writing is tiny. The size of writing is the second most important clue to the personality of the subject.

The person whose writing is tiny may be an artist or a writer. This individual probably pays a lot of attention to small details. Writing like this shows that the writer is not wasting energy on anything but his or her main aim in life. This may result in the subject becoming annoyed or irritated by small matters.

Please come to our book fair.
It starts April 1 and ends April 5.

small writing

Small writing tells of a person who is an intellectual. This person may be a scholar, a teacher, a philosopher, or a statesman. Even if the subject is not one of these, he or she still is an intelligent observer with the ability to lead others.

Average-sized writing tells of the average person—but that is not the whole story. This person is well balanced and may have a great deal of ability. Pay attention to the other

Mary had a little lamb.
Its fleece was white as snow,

average-sized writing

factors in the analysis and you may find that the subject could do well in business by himself or herself. The writer could be an inventor or a scientist.

Large writing tells of a person who is very active and some-

Abraham Lincoln was
a great president.

large writing

times restless. This subject may want constant change and may desire to control others, but can be generous and self-confident. But he or she had better concentrate on doing instead of talking.

Mary had a little
lamb

huge writing

Huge writing is the mark of the conceited person. He or she may have big ideas, but cannot put up with criticism. On the other hand, huge writing is a sign of honesty.

Along with the size of writing, some graphologists like to look at the width of the writing stroke. A thick stroke is the sign

I thought it was good.
Hope to see you here.

thick stroke

of greediness. A thin stroke means that the subject is not interested in love. A medium, firm stroke signifies energy, but the subject can be temperamental.

ANGLES OF WRITING

The third characteristic of writing is easily spotted. It is the angle of writing, and can be of seven types, depending on the angle. Here is a diagram that can be used to judge the angle:

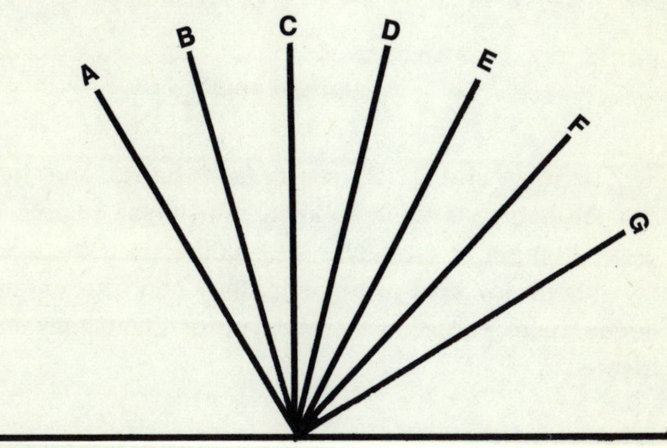

The person with a backward angle (A and B) lives in the past. He or she is often distrustful of others, very reserved, cold, and often timid. Here is a fear of facing the world or confronting present problems. It also tells of an unthinking per-

Mary had a little lamb
Its fleece was white as snow

backward angle

son, at least as far as being considerate of others is concerned.

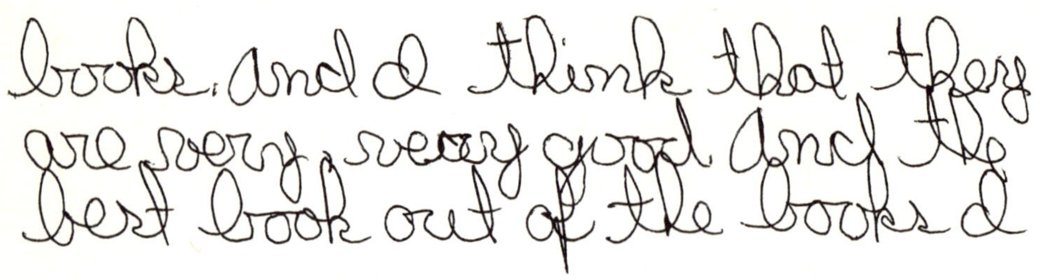

upright angle

Upright writing (C) shows selfishness and insensitivity. But the subject's mind is keen. And these people may have great strength of character and judgment. Although they may be without any kind of emotion, they can also be sincere and dependable. People with this type of angle may make good friends.

I'm at the library right now
taking a study break I've been
here all afternoon with no breaks

normal angle

The person with a normal angle (D) is easygoing, friendly, calm, and sensitive. But don't depend on this. Many people use this angle when they are trying to make their writing readable, and therefore it might not be their usual angle.

The person with a forward angle (E) is generous and sensitive to others. Also, tender to the point where the heart rules the head, so the subject may be extra susceptible to the ideas of others. This subject has a desire to spread happiness. All of this means that he or she may be overly sentimental and

apparently interested in
talking about there's an

forward angle

probably can be easily taken advantage of. Here is a person who may lack willpower, but is kind.

The person with the far-forward angle (F and G) is often nervous and high-strung, as well as impressionable. He or she lacks good reasoning abilities and is too sensitive. Temper

I like to get away by
myself at times.

far-forward angle

tantrums are common. You must be careful when analyzing the writing of this sort of person. The subject may become too excited for comfort.

Some people's writing has mixed angles. This can be a bad sign. These people are unable to face facts. There is a struggle between their hearts and their heads. And they find decision-making very uncomfortable.

LINE SPACING

The next trait in handwriting is also easy to observe. It is line spacing. There are four types—close, average, wide, and even.

I go to Garden Home School.
What skhools have you gone to?

close spacing

Lines that are close together look messy. And the mind of the writer can also be cluttered. This is the writing of a person who wants to say a lot and thinks that there is not enough space in which to say it. It is also a sign of greediness. This subject may be a rapid talker.

Lines that are average in spacing show a calm person. He or she deals with problems as they arise and does not try too hard to influence other people. This is usually a good

and father. I really dont believe that.
and said he had long white teeth
to. Please write back and if it

average spacing

sign, but it might also mean that the subject tends to be too easygoing.

Wide spacing can fool you. Many people believe that wide spacing indicates a fine mind because many great men and women have had handwriting that was widely spaced. But it also may be true that since the great ones have been writing on great subjects, they have been extra careful about their

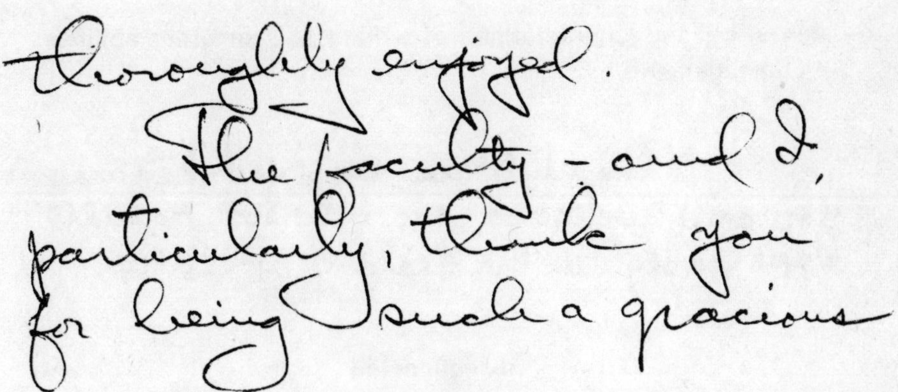

wide spacing

writing in order to be understood. Wide spacing does indicate a feeling of importance—sometimes conceit. It also tells of a liberal mind, full of great care and caution.

Even spacing, no matter whether the spaces are close, average, or wide, tells of good judgment and a big imagination. If the spaces are not consistent, the subject is of an uncertain mind.

LETTER SPACING

Before you examine the letter spacing within each word, look at the space between the words. Words are spaced either evenly or unevenly. If there is equal space between words, the subject is calm and rational. If the spaces between words are uneven, the subject is impulsive.

If the letters within each word are connected, the subject is firm and exact. He or she is good at solving problems, and intelligent in making decisions. This also may be a sign of suspicion. The subject is impatient with people who make mistakes, but this characteristic of writing tells of great abilities in management.

The children enjoyed hearing you and we have seen direct results especially in the field of pollution.

disconnected

If the letters within each word are sometimes disconnected, the subject will take chances. This is because he or she is often a good judge of character and a person with a lot of intuition. This is a sign of talent and inspiration.

I have always liked to visit Indiana. The people

very disconnected

If the letters within each word are very disconnected (but not printed), the subject uses intuition instead of thought and lives in a dream world. It is the sign of the poet and the nature lover.

Cramped writing, where the letters are crowded together, shows that the subject hates wastefulness. Obviously, here is a cautious person, especially when it comes to money. Al-

Abraham Lincoln was a great president.

cramped writing

though this may mean that the subject is a keen business man or woman, he or she probably is quite suspicious of others, and may even be a miser.

My brother had a dream the other

spread writing

Spread writing, where the letters are far apart, tells of the free spender, the lover of a good time. This person is friendly, but he or she is also forgetful.

Now you have figured out a lot about your subjects, and you can stop here. But if you want to know more, you have to go on to the fine points of graphology.

The Fine Points

Some graphologists say that the "fine points" count more in the analysis than all of the things that you have learned in the "quick-glance" method. The fine points, they say, are specific. The quick-glance items are general. Let's take a look at the fine points.

LETTER FORMATIONS

There are three main types of letter formations—rounded letters, angular writing, and block writing.

Rounded letters are just that—rounded. Here is a person who has an even temper and is gentle with others. He or she also has a desire for harmony and comfort. But the subject is often lazy and wants too much luxury.

Angular writers are just the opposite. They are energetic and get things done. Naturally, they are aggressive. They are also very impatient leaders. They want quick results. By the way, they are hardly ever very artistic.

Block writing is the sign of practicality. Here is a person

who is very careful and painstaking—the steady worker who is hardly ever inspired. Many people with this type of writing have home workshops, and they may even earn a living as accountants or in some other job that requires a great deal of care.

LETTER VARIATIONS

Exact letters come in two sizes. There are small letters, such as *a* and *e,* and large letters, such as *h* and *f.* But writing containing exact letters is writing where all the small letters are the same size, and all the large letters are the same size, although larger than the small letters. This type of writing tells of a conscientious person, a direction-follower, a perfectionist.

Irregular letters are letters that change from small to large or from large to small, as the person writes. If they change back and forth in the same line, the subject is fickle and will take the easy way out of a situation. But he or she may be clever and ready to try anything new. If the letters start small and become larger at the end of the line, you have a person who is happy to express himself or herself. This person is ambitious and hardworking. If the letters start large and get smaller as the line goes on, you have a person who has a lot of tact and is a good listener—fair and friendly.

OPEN AND SHUT LETTERS

Take a look at such letters as the *a* and the *o.* These can be either open or shut at the top. Open letters show an open mind. They are signs of a person who is confident, but who may be thoughtless, frank, and outspoken. Shut letters show a closed mind, but these people have definite opinions that they can keep to themselves. If the subject uses both open and shut letters, he or she is friendly, but can keep a secret. Also, this person is trusting at some times and suspicious at others.

SPECIAL LETTER VARIATIONS

If you have a lot of time for your analysis, you will probably want to go over the sample letter by letter. These special letter variations can give you more information about your subject. (*A* and *c* are not considered important.) The list is long, but the information can be important. Let's take the lowercase letters first.

b with big loop—kindness and understanding
with small loop—a real individual
with no loop—determination

d with big loop—timid, easily managed
short letter—crafty
tall letter—idealistic
looks like a musical note—ambition
leaning backward—intellect
curved forward—self-centered
wide letter—quiet, able to keep a secret

e rounded—natural personality
narrow letter—unsure of oneself
Greek letter (ε)—conceit, a show-off

f fancy letter—self-sufficient
small loop—accurate and precise
long letter below the line—active nature
short letter below the line—physically weak

g shaped like the number 8—big vocabulary, likes to read
with straight downstroke—scientific
rounded below the line—fanciful
with small loop—a tyrant

h with high loop—imagination and understanding
with low loop—businesslike

i with no dot—negligence
with light dot—easily influenced

with heavy dot—coarse, blunt, aggressive
with circular dot—affectation
with dot over letter—careful, orderly, methodical
with dot to the right of letter—a quick mind
with dot to the left of letter—slow thinking
with high dot—imagination, mysticism
with low dot—practical, painstaking
with stroked dot—impatience
with dot like a comma—mental ability
with square, thick dot—desire for possessions
letter pointed like upside-down *v*—eagerness

j with dot to the right of letter—a quick mind
with dot to the left of letter—slow thinking
rounded below the line—fanciful

k with high loop—exaggeration

l with high loop—exaggeration
with narrow loop—exacting
with normal loop—balanced nature
small letter that looks like an *e*—hasty, lack of thought

m well-rounded letter—precision
angular letter—friendly

n well-rounded letter—precision
angular letter—friendly

o letter that looks like an *a*—unsystematic

p with high loop—imagination
with slight loop—practical
letter that looks like an *h*—traditional

q with long loop below the line—fanciful
ornamental letter—pays attention to detail

r well-formed letter—careful and precise
rounded letter—lacks inspiration

angular letter—intellect
letter that looks like printed *r*—expressive.

s letter extra-large—tends to be excessive
sloppy letter—energetic and talkative
printed letter—greedy
large printed letter—dominating

t simple letter—balanced
small, simple letter—average intelligence
looped—oversensitive
pointed—bluntness
with low cross—submits to others
with high cross—strong will
with cross halfway up—calm and thoughtful
with cross above letter—dominating, demanding
with cross curved above the letter—oppressive
with thin cross—kindly and careful
with heavy cross—violence
with cross to left of letter—hesitation
with cross to right of letter—initiative
with cross thicker at one end—coarseness
with short cross—lack of willpower
with long cross—impatience
with rising cross—argumentative
with rising, curving cross—quibbling
with descending cross—obstinacy
with descending, curving cross—obstinacy
with no cross—ill will
letter formed in one stroke—hastiness

u letter looks like an *n*—easygoing
letter is well-rounded—overly careful
letter is pointed—overeager to be liked

v letter shaped like a *u*—overly refined
letter ends high at right—conscientious

w letter is angular—sociable
letter is well-rounded—takes pains
letter has low center stroke—efficiency

x curved, with short straight cross—hasty
sharp, with long cross—forceful

y with straight downstroke—firm and rugged
with rounded loop below line—fanciful

z with rounded loop below line—fanciful
letter is printed—careful of details

Then you can go on with the capital letters. First read them in terms of style.

Simple, or "old-style" (with twists and flourishes) capitals show intellect, practicality, and reliability. The less graceful they are, the less the intellect. The more graceful they are, the greater the taste and artistic sense of the subject.

Printed capitals are a sign of an artistic mind and include skills. But if they are rigid, there is a suggestion of mechanical or scientific interests.

Graceful capitals show ambition and an interest in new ideas.

Ornate capitals, with flourishes and curves, indicate an overly proud person with a great deal of conceit—in short, pretension and ostentation.

Small capitals of about the size of the small letters indicate excessive modesty.

Large capitals show a vain person, perhaps even boastful. And the larger the letters, the more overbearing the person.

Here are a few more things you might look for in general:

Capitals closely written—timidity
Capitals large and open—a bluffer
Capitals large at the bottom—practicality
Capitals large at the top—vanity

Capitals "on stilts"—self-sufficiency
Capitals underlining the following letters—self-satisfaction
Capitals covering the following letters—too much pride
Capitals with hooks at beginning—greediness
Capitals with hooks at both ends—avarice
Capitals connecting with next letter—forgetfulness
Capitals of mixed types—adaptability

Finally, you can read the capitals by looking at specific letters.

A beginning with a hook—grasping
beginning and ending with a hook—greedy

D ending with a hook, upper left—critical

H letter is wide—strong and decisive
letter is narrow—lack of confidence, shyness

M with very high first stroke—vanity, boastfulness
with high first stroke—independence
with equal height strokes—urge for culture, but short on ambition
with strokes that descend like stairs—pessimism
with strokes that go up like stairs—ambition
with three downstrokes—aristocratic
with two downstrokes—obstinacy
beginning with a hook—grasping
beginning and ending with a hook—boastful
with rounded strokes—gentleness
with angular strokes—obstinacy
strokes joined halfway up—greed

Now that you know what to look for, have some fun with these handwriting samples:

Hi Fran

How is New York these days. I know about the bad polution. I hope you had a good time down here and I was so glad to see you, that I cried when you left home. Everthing is alright down here. School is O.K but the Lesson isn't that bad but it isn't all that easy. You told me to write you and tell you how much the Mini Bike cost. The best ones cost about $225.

But that not the only reason I wrote you. I wanted to here from you. I really hope you be able to buy me one cause

February 11, 1976
[illegible] HI

Barbra,

Hi, hows it going? Well and good for us. I'm sorry that its taking me so long to write and give you some of our cheers. Anyways, here's my favorite ones.

(Football cheers)

Mighty Brownies

We are the Mighty Brownies,
Our aim is to Succeed.
Our power is strong, we cant go wrong
Our power is best,
We'll meet the test
Brownies Best!

Victory

Victory Brownies, win tonight
Show your courage,
prove your might.
V-I-C-T-O-R-Y Brownies
Alright!

I Love Mini Bikes. Daddy said that he would buy me one but he don't have the ~~[illegible]~~ Money cause he has to pay all the bills. I like bicicles but I lik Mini Bikes better. Thats all for know and I'll write again.

Love Sandy
your brother

P.S. Auburn-10
TENNSSEE-9

Signatures

No matter how often graphologists point out that the signature is not such a good thing to analyze, people still want to analyze signatures. So we must consider how this is done in order for you to get the most fun out of your new hobby.

But remember that you are playing a game. If words are important (and they are), then writing is important as a way to communicate. The written word stands for a thing or a feeling. So what is the most important specimen of handwriting to a person? His or her name.

Hardly anyone has a signature that looks like the rest of his or her writing. We have all prettied up our written names to express what we think is our personality.

Anyway, here are the rules for reading a signature. Just don't go overboard.

The signature followed by a period or a dash tells of a cautious person. It indicates a great deal of prudence, to the point of being afraid of what others might think. The subject may also be secretive or suspicious.

The signature followed by a stroke is the sign of a distrustful person. The subject is always on guard and uses any trick possible to get his or her own way.

The signature ending with a downstroke that looks like a sword tells of a defensive person. If the downstroke looks like a club, it stands for stern defense. If it looks like a harpoon, it means violent defense.

The signature ending with a flourish that looks like a knife tells of a combative fighter. If the flourish ends in a point, the subject is aggressive and militant. An up-and-down flourish that thickens is a sign of willpower. If it gets thinner, the trait is combativeness. If the flourish looks like a harpoon, the writer is tenacious.

The shieldlike flourish looks as though it is used to protect the good name of the writer, and it stands for courage. But if it droops off on the end, it means caution.

A backstroke without a curve at the end of the signature tells of a defensive person who can bear a grudge.

An underlining stroke with a hook at the end stands for pride with skill.

A backstroke with several angular return lines tells that the subject is energetic and a fighter. Also, this person is bound to try to get his or her own way.

A zigzagging, lightninglike backstroke is the sign of an active and self-willed person.

Rounded zigzags tell of gentleness. Angular zigzags are signs of rigidity. Both of these have to do with willpower.

The backstroke that forms gentle curves tells that the writer is cheerful and good-natured.

If the backstroke looks like a cowboy's rope with knots in it, it means great skill. But if the lassos cross each other, the writer likes intrigue.

The backstroke that looks like a corkscrew is a sign of cunning.

When the flourish looks like a knotted necktie, we have a person with tact and skill in negotiations.

The cobweb flourish indicates commercial or business ability.

The picket-fence flourish stands for distrust.

The flourish that almost surrounds the signature tells of a subject who is egotistical and demands satisfaction.

The flourish that surrounds the name stands for an unhappy person.

If there is no flourish at all, the subject is rather ordinary.

So much for the flourishes and decorations. Let's look at some of the other points having to do with the signature.

The extremely large signature, at least twice the size of the normal writing, without flourishes, means pride, intelligence, self-confidence, and even a royal nature.

The medium-sized signature, without any flourishes, stands for simplicity and a quiet self-confidence.

The signature that is the same size as the rest of a person's writing—one that almost looks like the regular handwriting—means moderation. Here is a person who is a clear thinker and is the same in private as in public.

The up-and-down signature that goes with a slanted handwriting tells of a person who is cool in public. However, he or she may be warm and loving in private.

The signature whose first letter is much larger than the rest of the name is often a sign of great pride. But check this out. If there is a letter *i* in the name and it is very small, you have a person who is trying to overcome an inferiority complex.

The signature that is very clear, legible, and utterly readable signifies a desire to be understood and a personality that can be extremely loyal.

The signature that is completely unreadable tells of a desire for secrecy. It also may be the sign of an eccentric person.

The ascending signature is the mark of an ambitious, optimistic person.

The descending signature shows fatigue and often discouragement.

The signature with a separate simple line under it signifies pride and self-confidence.

The signature with a separate simple line over it (this may be a part of the signature as the cross on a capital *T*) is the sign of a selfish person. He or she may also be self-protective.

The signature with both separate simple lines is the sign of a selfish, cold, mistrustful egotist.

The signature with a separate wavy line under it signifies a graceful, witty person. He or she may also be flirtatious.

The signature written to the left of the center of the page tells of a person with little self-confidence.

The signature placed to the right of the page is the sign of a lack of common sense.

So much for the unusual things that you can find in signatures. You can attack the rest of the letters in the name in the same way that you analyze them in normal writing.

Edgar A Poe

This is the signature of Edgar Allan Poe, the great American poet, short-story writer, and novelist. Poe started out thinking of the military life and even attended West Point for a time. But his main love was writing, and almost every American has read some of his works: the poem "The Raven," for example, or the short story "The Fall of the House of Usher." He is given credit for being the inventor of the detective story. His life, however, was a sad one.

Before reading the traits in his signature, we should remember that Poe himself was an amateur handwriting analyst, and this may have affected his signature. However, we can see pride in the large signature, as well as intelligence and self-confidence. The large first letter also tells of pride, as does the separate line under the signature. This line also reinforces the trait of self-confidence. It is a clear but complex signature, which indicates a desire to be understood (a good trait for a writer) and yet to be understood in a complex way (and many of his stories and poems are complex).

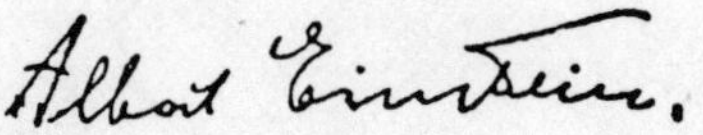

This is the signature of Albert Einstein, one of the most brilliant mathematicians and scientists of all time. His work on relativity made him so famous that his name became a synonym for intellectual brilliance. Yet he was a humble man, perhaps because he was a failure in school during his early life and because he escaped from Hitler's Germany during the days of the persecution of the Jews.

The period after the signature tells of a cautious, prudent man who is afraid of what others may think. Caution and prudence are two of the most important traits of the scientist. The letters are the same size, telling of moderation and clear thinking, but a person who is the same in public as in private. Since the signature is neither extremely clear nor unreadable, here we have a normally adjusted man.

This is the signature of Marlin Perkins, who has been extremely successful in two careers. He was an outstanding director of the Lincoln Park Zoo in Chicago for many years and later moved to St. Louis as the director of the zoo there. But he is probably better known as the host of the award-winning television program *Mutual of Omaha's Wild Kingdom,* in which he takes the viewer to all parts of the world by means of nature films.

While the lack of a flourish may seem to mark him as an ordinary man, and the medium-sized signature tells of simplicity, these two items can also indicate self-confidence. This is a trait necessary for those who are in charge of others and especially for those who appear before the public. The first letter is large, indicating pride. And the signature is clear, which tells of a desire to be understood—very valuable for the host of an educational program. The ascending nature of the writing tells of ambition (he was famous in two different lines of work) and optimism (a TV star must be optimistic).

This is the signature of Melvin Van Peebles, the writer, composer, director, producer, actor, and singer. One of his films was an award-winner at the San Francisco Film Festival. His Broadway plays have received nine Tony nominations. And he has recorded many record albums. Add to that the fact that he has written eight books, and we all must agree with Clive Barnes, drama critic of *The New York Times,* that Van Peebles "is a man for all seasons."

This is a large signature without flourishes, which tells of pride, intelligence, and self-confidence. All of these traits are essential to a public performer. The trait of pride is emphasized by the large first letters of the names. It is a clear signature, indicating a desire to be understood (important for a writer) and a sense of loyalty (important to an actor or a musician).

This is the signature of Jackie Jensen, the coach of the University of California, Berkeley, baseball team. While he was in college, he was named All-American in both baseball and football. After graduation he played major league baseball for eleven years, and in 1958, while with the Red Sox, hit thirty-five home runs and was named the most valuable player in the American League.

The harpoon-shaped flourish that gets thinner tells us that he is tenacious and combative—two traits that are necessary to the big-time athlete. The writing, the same size as his regular script, tells us of his moderation and ability to think clearly. These traits are invaluable to the coach. The first letter is much larger than the rest, showing pride, and the signature is easily read, showing loyalty. These two attributes are vital to the coach or the team player.

Feeling Lucky?

There is really no reason for including this chapter except to let you have a little fun with your friends. Foretelling luck or the lack of it is not a part of graphology. But you can pretend. Here is a little table of luck:

Signs of Good Luck

Lines slanting upward
Crossing of the *t* high or upward
Letters connected and clear
Wide margins
The *o* and *a* open
Dots on the *i* well marked
Round, regular, legible writing
Writing without backward hooks
Upright or slightly sloping writing

Signs of Bad Luck

Lines slanting downward
Missing *t* cross

Crossing of the *t* low or sloping downward
Letters disconnected and badly shaped
Lack of margins
The *o* and *a* closed
Dots on the *i* badly marked
Angular, squat, or illegible writing
Writing with backward hooks
Backward or extremely sloping writing

But before you think that this list is a supernatural one, take a look at some things. The traits in the bad-luck column are those of pessimistic people who lack willpower and ideas. These people are also egotistical and coarse. The traits that are included in the good-luck column are the traits of optimistic, intelligent, frank, good persons. These people are not egotistical. It doesn't take a fortune-teller to know which people have the best chance of being successful.

Bibliography

Gardner, Martin. *Fads and Fallacies in the Name of Science.* New York: Dover Publications, 1957.

Gibson, Walter B., and Gibson, Litzka R. *The Complete Illustrated Book of the Psychic Sciences.* Garden City, N.Y.: Doubleday & Co., 1966.

Poinset, M. C., ed. *The Encyclopedia of Occult Sciences.* New York: Tudor Publishing Co., 1968.

de Sainte Colombe, Paul. *Grapho-Therapeutics.* Hollywood, Calif.: Laurinda Books Publishing Co., 1966.

Watson, Lyall. *Supernature.* Garden City, N.Y.: Doubleday & Co., 1973.

Index

About the Author

Graphology is Tom Aylesworth's twenty-first book. Usually his biography says he has a Ph.D., once taught science at the university level, and is presently an editor with a major New York City publishing company. Here are some other facts about him that you may find interesting: Hobbies—sailing (he has a twenty-one-foot sailboat and uses it on Long Island Sound), music (he plays the clarinet, guitar, and marimba), and travel (he has visited fourteen countries).

This is my best.

Strange Tree

Away Beyond the Garboe house
I saw a different kind of
tree,
Its bark old large, and
bent,
And I could feel it look at
me

The road was going on and on
Beyond to reach some other
place
I saw a tree that looked at
me and yet it didn't have
a face.

Barbara,

How have you been? I am doing great. I have a new boyfriend. His name is David. He'll be up your way next week. How's Melvin or whoever it is now? By the way, who is it. How's Mario? Tell him hello.

I am really exicited about starting school. We start on Sept 23. I am getting a grant for $326 and I have about $300 savings and I am suppposed to get some more aid from the school so I hope to go to school off that. It comes to about 900 so I may have enough saved from the fall & winter to pay for the spring quarter without borr-owing any money. I refuse to go to the Credit Union. I don't think Mom and Dad will have to give me more

644 Matt Leonard Drive
B'ham, Alabama. 35211

We hold these Truths...
UNITED STATES 10c

Ms. H. Walker
1738 Columbus Ave #10B
New York, N.Y. 10024